I0518376

Ayeesha's

Poetry
Collection

Ayeesha S. Kanji

Executive Press Ltd
Edmonton AB T6A 0H7
Canada
343-554-1210

The views expressed in this work are solely those of the author and
do not necessarily reflect the views of the publisher, and the publisher
hereby disclaims any responsibility for them.

Paperback ISBN: 979-8-9931291-0-5
Ebook ISBN: 979-8-9931291-1-2

Ayeesha's Poetry Collection

Ayeesha S. Kanji

To the three people who have always supported my dreams and believed in me, thank you always for everything you have done for me. Letting me grow up on my own timeline and supporting me through my choices is the only thing I could ever ask for. To my mom, brother and Dad (in spirit), I am blessed and beyond grateful for all of you. Thank you, every day, for everything.

A portion of the proceeds from this book will be donated to
Aga Khan Foundation Canada

Contents

A Cup of Coffee

It's amazing what coffee tastes like

I was sitting there in the hostel
The cup small enough to hold espresso
Had a handle big enough for two fingers

The smell, taste and feel of it
I can still describe
It was so amazing because
I have tasted the worst coffee ever

When I sipped it, I could smell the roasting of the fresh
coffee beans and feel the taste all over my body I could
taste the aroma as it warmed me, as I was about to
embark on the most romantic city in the world
The smell of hot and fresh French baguette
complemented my taste buds

I sat there enjoying an amazing cup of coffee

Found in Paris, France
Other Places
Tim Hortons
Facility Coffee
Second Cup
The Coffee Bean
Starbucks
McDonalds
Dunkin' Donuts
Seattle's Best Coffee
Timothy's Coffee
Rooster Coffee House

I'm happy to say
I love what coffee tastes like
Tastes, feels, and smells like
Because it is found
In a place far from me

Sitting in Paris, France
Is where I'd rather be
Thank God I am me
To say that coffee is as important as me

A Time of Gratitude

It's that time of year

The malls are insane
The parking lots are a mess
You missed by a day being charged 20% on your credit
card holiday debt
But really....
Is it about being busy.....or
Being grateful?

Let's review the time of the year for gratitude

A time to be thankful for the gift of life
A time to be thankful for hard work, party hard and
no drama
A time to be grateful for the people who respect your
time, space and energy
A time to remember all the souls who shine and watch
over you daily and to be grateful for the memories you
have of them
A time to remember your lessons, experiences, funny
moments and be grateful for how it has shaped who you
have become

It's the time of year to smile, to love, and to reflect
The holidays mean different things for everyone
But the collective feeling of gratitude translates into
an amazing thing....
An abundance of happiness to share with everyone
around you

Always

The pitter patter of little feet
Learning a new language

A smile beautiful like a diamond
Laughter which allows your heart to skip a beat

Crying louder than glass breaking
A symbol of innocence

A reason why it is worth to live
A soul who chooses from above

A gift from God
The meaning of being a woman
When a woman is born again
When the miracle of life is inside
When a baby comes into your life
It is like a miracle is given to you

It is a moment to treasure
A moment to hold on to
A moment you have to yourself

Treasure your moment, your miracle, yourself

Always

Angel

Look over me
Guide me through
Through the life
Without you

Guard me by
Your wings of love
Love in my heart
To hold me high

Shower blessings
To make me smile
Smile even when
I can't get by

Protect my life
From the vex world
World unknown

As my own life may be

Be by my side, as the days go by
Shine your light, strong as it can be
For me to believe

Beautiful Day

A beautiful day means......

No stress
No need to be productive
Feeling well rested
Feeling strong

A beautiful day means.....

No deadlines
No commitments
No meetings

A beautiful day.......

Is a day
With yourself

And

Nobody else

Being

In the moment
In your presence

With myself
Watching sunrise

Happy without
The need for things

Sad over
The chaotic world

Just being

Being me

As reality bites me

Being myself
As I cry
As I am happy
As I live each moment

Being underneath
The pale blue sky
As someone might think of me
As someone may want to hold me

Being in this world
Is more than
My physical presence

Mind, body and soul
Is to be
All of me

All of me
Alone or not
In this crazy world
We know to be
Reality

Catch The Sun

"I like that
What is it?
Why can't I catch it?
My hand was right there!
I'm smiling because I want that.
It makes me smile.
Whatever it is.
I feel warm.
It looks cool.
Why can't I catch it?
I'm sitting in the best spot.
I can't say her name.
But she's fun!
I'll sleep really well tonight! My
hand is right there, ready,
Awwwwww man, I didn't catch it!"

My cousin's son, sat on my lap
He saw the sun
The light warm on his face
Glowing into his space of warmth
He will know one day
He wanted to catch the sun
How amazing is that
To catch what Mother Nature blesses us with
Next time I see the sun, I will catch it, and you can too

It's in your heart, your mind and your eyes
It's the feeling of warmth, love and happiness
Be a kid and embrace the playfulness within you
Catch the sun before life catches up in a game with you!

Dancing

Dancing is more than just the act of moving, or performing and even choreography. It is the act of moving through life with a beat and knowing when to stop, knowing when the dance is over and knowing whether or not the move is right. It is known to be the poetry of movement.

I make sense to myself when I think the way I do but to others this all might be a load of words on nothing. Is a professional dancer merely a trained individual who dances, choreographs, and smiles to hide their nervous attitude? Or is a professional dancer an individual who performs, analyzes, choreographs, acts and believes that whether fast or slow, where there is a beat there is a dance? Defining what a dancer is or a professional dancer is may not suit certain aspects.

Dancing itself comes from the heart, dancing is more than just knowledge, teaching and most importantly, dancing is more than what you wear and how you smile for an audience.

Dancing conditions me in all three ways: mentally, spiritually and physically. It builds my confidence, clears my head and uplifts my spirits to help me be a stronger person in my daily life. I have learnt many forms of dancing.

I dance my way through life. My silent quiet nights reflect that the beat has stopped and that the melody does not fit. When I am at work, it is the rhythm of my routine that I live by. My nights on the town are the hook of the melody, or of the story that is being performed as I feel it, in my heart, eyes and soul.

Not a moment passes now, or in the past about how much I realize as to how much I love dancing and how much it does for me. I dance in each moment I live; I dance for each emotion I feel and I dance to the joys of life, the joys within me and the joys of dancing, always.

Energy

All the marks on me are just a feeling
The feeling of being broken yet whole
The feeling of silence in a cold room
The feeling of energy waiting to burst
The feeling of warm, fresh, crisp air flowing through
my hair

It's the reminder of what energy means
Kick, push, get it done

Flowing through me day and night
Stride and strut, walk it out

Why is my energy constantly changing
So, what if I have more than one head twenty times
in a day

All my marks are a feeling
I still stand; I still can do what I need to do
But it's time for a recharge
As I patiently wait

My energy is marked until I kick, push into full gear

Bring me back to life, bring my energy back

So, I don't feel the marks

On my back

Exhale

Exhilarate
X-Factor
Human
Angelic
Loving
Energy

Fade

Engulf me
To help me see you
So I know you
Between me and you

The water is still
As I am
Like that of
A tree

Unknowingly
You came to me
In the wind
Circling
Amongst me

You say you love me
So why is it
Not strong like
The way
I love me?

Can you uplift me
To the heavens above
With your mind
While making love to me?

Engulf me
So I know you

And just when I do

You fade away

Feminine

I am strong
    And also sensitive

I am willing
    And also scared

I am caring
    And also unethical

I am nurturing
    And also inconsiderate

I am gentle
    And also tough

Did I mention

I am

Feminine?

Friendship

A theory, a concept or a gem as it is known in life. A line of support between two people. An irreplaceable sense of security with a person whose actions are not predictable and a relationship where emotions are not based on obligation, but understanding. A bond based on support, trust and honesty. A bond for lifetime because acquaintances come and go. Time is not ever an issue but given and received always at the drop of a hat. Distance and change do not define it. It is a real concept, not fake but togetherness at heart. The true unconditional love that lasts despite the past. It can be recent, or from childhood or high school, but that line of connection still remains. The theories of friendship are endless. A connection can last forever, just as a friendship can be just as better. When you believe in what you want, you will have it forever.

Goddess

An innate being of nature, of a connection with the ultimate root of an apple

A woman of substance, of being in her spirit, mentally and physically in each moment she lives

A person of an intertwined mind of love, happiness, security, self-acceptance and sensuality

A goddess is a connection intertwined in substance and in being with one-self

Although not restricted to the type of woman, the concept is a form of beauty that exists within the heart and mind

I know a goddess
I woke up to reality
I am a voice of reason
I am a voice of emotion
I am a voice of beauty
I symbolize

Self-Acceptance
Sexuality
Love

I acknowledge my goddess
At this moment
I know now
My seed of inspiration

The goddess within me
The goddess I am meant to be
The goddess I love to be

I love to be

Me

Grass

Firm and clean, cut with precision—patches scattered,
bushes in corners, sometimes dry, sometimes lush.
Decorated with dirt, leaves, and trees, the surface gets
smooshed or soaked.

Still, grass endures. Even in the cold, it doesn't
surrender.
Surrounded by humanity—buildings, people,
animals—it never complains.
You can lay a blanket down, nap under the sky, or
simply admire the view.
God's creation, often overlooked when neglected.

Water gives strength. Air brings life.
Fields, backyards, and hidden corners are shaped by
its presence.
Soft beneath your feet, even when damp.
Creatures hide. Children play. Adults fire up the grill.
Summer brings warmth, fall comfort, winter chills, and
spring revival.

Earth's living carpet, stretching far and wide.
One color, never plain. Picking blades, tossing them—
it's all part of the joy.

Often seen as background, yet placed with purpose.
There's complexity beneath its simplicity like life itself.
Grass—layered, resilient, and deeper than we think

Gravity

Angel you are gravity are you not?

You uplift as space and gravity would when I ask of
you to guide me
You are my energy always with me like an mp3 on my
phone

I hold your beads
I know no matter what
A moment does not pass without your spirit in my
breath

Invisible you are gravity like in space it's belief that
allows you to carry
Invisible you are gravity like in love carrying you in
every moment of just being
Invisible you are gravity like in Mother Nature who
only exists through a child
Gravity, you are my angel, angel, you are gravity,
invisible, equal and pure

As the sun warms over me and a breeze flows through
my hair. I am left with one question…

Pink, purple, red, black…when do I get yellow, I want
yellow.

He Loves Me, He Loves Me Not....

With each petal the saying is...he loves me, he loves me not

How this came about I do not know...what I do know, is that love is not that simple or easy

It's not always soft or even pretty...it can fall a part or even not grow as fast

Some old tradition stated the petals of a flower tell you if your love is true or not

Or is it a game between friends to see who can win based on the number of petals...

Are there rules, can I think of two men and change the name for each petal...

I don't know, I can try now...

I'm a princess waiting for that one love to love me the way I love myself...

Maybe the petals can count all the wrong ones to see how many I have left before that one comes along...

That makes more sense...

Not he loves me, he loves me not, but he didn't work, he didn't work, but maybe he will...

So when you pull each petal, the amount left shows how many more are left before the one...

He didn't want me, neither did he, but then maybe he will...

That sounds better because I know one thing...

I love myself first, not someone else...

Image

My soul is on fire as I sit silent in the sky. The promises you made unaware of the disaster, which would unfold. The memories I hold of your breath in control of my spirit. My heart as faithful as I was to you, was stealing your eyes in the moment we held. The color of my shadow when you worshipped me was fate, as destiny controls our lives. The world we live in prompts intentions, which we become unaware of as happiness fades away. As I gaze to this world you are supposedly in, my image subsides. For my image, is all I have left.

Marriage

They looked at each other
Two people as one
Hand in hand
Till death do they apart

To a commitment
Of honesty, trust
Unconditional Love
Under a union blessed
By their hearts

Only in their eyes
Is the love seen
What brought them as one
From one moment
That changed their lives

Today as they stand
Accepting each other
Uttering "I Do"
A solidified union

This is a commitment for life

Muse

She was a muse on fire. The seeds she planted were in waves and in the nude. Was she a muse grown up and sticking to the norm? No. Was she a muse drawn out of her fakeness to maintain realness? Yes.

She is her own passion project. In a model moment she validates herself of her straightforward mind, her straightforward being. All that glitters around her is just a feeling.

Music

Put me in the mood
To make me move

Even when
It makes me cry
When it gets
To my heart

I laugh when
It makes me happy

My life, my soul
Music is food
To my soul

The only universal language in this world is music. It allows a way for artists to express themselves in a way that even as humans we cannot express our own feelings in such a manner.

Music provokes emotions that at times are surprising; you can say happiness or sadness; it is a sense of being with yourself or at times hearing another story. Music is a treasure in life. At times, I will sit with a CD or a record, open the book leaflet or the record cover and just read the words along with each song.

I feel productive when I do, with my thoughts enveloped in the rhythm of each beat or the melody of the notes. Sometimes the words are so beautiful, I'm inspired to write my own poems. So, in that case, music is food to my soul in life as it inspires me to believe and to write. No color, no violence and no room to blame. Owning the freedom to express thoughts and your innermost feelings. Expression without limits is why music is the universal language of the world, nothing else in this world like it, not now, not ever.

My New York Poem

Space is breath. It is deep, small, long and in spurts.

It's called life.

Space is breath not just a moment to yourself.

It's when you admit that the scars of your past shape who you become but do not define you.

Time always controls us; but why don't we control time, why don't we actually just breathe, or actually just live?

Open, create and allow permission.

We all have a right to think but overdoing it is the easiest thing anyone can do.

Crammed in between a busy schedule, how often do we give ourselves space?

Karma or you could say the law of attraction is what determines what you receive in this world.

Measure your space - break your patterns, use your mistakes to grow and take your own advice.

Knowledge is power, come out of your shell and accept your fears.

It's easier to think about yesterday, worry about tomorrow than to be present now.

Sucked into my dream, I allow myself permission to breath.

Stuck on the F train, I create my space.

Living on time, I open my mind.

Join me ... in my New York state of mind.

New York

I see New York

    And I smell possibility

I hear New York
    And I taste the hustling of life

I taste New York
    And I touch to just get by with pride

I smell New York
    And I hear I can do anything in the only city known
to be where dreams are made of

Life is now
As my third eye
Has awoken
In a purple sky
Life is now
In another New York Poem

Ocean

My heart is like an ocean. Surrounded with beauty, there is no limit to how much my heart can hold. As if each drop is within me to hold all the love, all the feelings and all the moments inside me. Does a river, lake or pond represent each feeling on its own? They say there is no limit to what a heart can hold but how much can a human being live to take or see of the scary world we live in?

Sea of Madness

This sea

Moves me around

To places I never been

And places I don't want

To be

It changes every so often

Goes east when I wanna

Go west

And is still when

I want

To move

This madness then takes me over

I figure

That's

LIFE

Soul

A clear view

Commonly with serenity

Allowing a sense of self-awareness to be seen within

The eyes of the beholder

Holding peaceful energy flowing within a light

A window of light, of inner beauty within anywhere of

A human's physical form

The eyes are the window

Eternally; it is with us always.

For its clarity writes reality.

SPIRIT

Fly away
Lift yourself up
And
Fly

Find it
Your inner strength

Find it
And fly

Find it

Your connection
With yourself and
And
Your connection with
Your beliefs and values

Fly away

Find it
Your inner peace

Who you are

Accept it
And fly

And when
You find it

Your spirit

Open up your heart
Look in the mirror

Whisper three words
I love you

True Love

Love is not always stronger than pride
As you get older you have more to lose
When you are young, love is blind and
Time is on your side

The cliché of what true love could ever be
Was an image as created or brainwashed by society
As impossible as it may seem
It's becoming a rarity

Love is built within a realm of
Fantasies and possibilities

Like in a fairy tale I have of you
Reality shows no happy ending
Friendship becomes the base and
Branches in different ways

The words of the song in my head
It's easier said than done, whether four beats in a bar
Or within a conversation
Pride saves your dignity
And who you are

If true love ever had existed
Then why do the clichés
Exist in mass popularity

If true love was and is possible
Then why is it hard so hard to
Make it real

If true love is within reach
Then why is it that the
Word love is so hard to define

True love is built more around
Patience, tolerance and understanding
Which come from communication?

True love is not the "zsa zsa zsu"
Exclusively separated from the other facets
Either you have both or you don't
You can't have it all or you'd not want more
True love can be without the "zsa zsa zsu"

I'm done

Done

Floating

Words

The song danced through my head,

The sound of light seen only in my mind.

A line can be forever.

A bright moment within a realm of possibilities

and is only dawn once a day.

A line can be forever.

The words

In my head will not stop, ever.

Nature is beautiful. It reminds us that we live in a world equally of chaos and beauty. Always count your blessings and remember that life is meant to be lived, not meant for anger and drama. One love.

Ayeesha S. Kanji

Photo taken in Cebu, Philippines